PIETRO ANTONIO LOCATELLI

L'ARTE DEL VIOLINO

Op. 3/5–8

Edited by/Herausgegeben von

Albert Dunning

Ernst Eulenburg Ltd

London · Mainz · Madrid · New York · Paris · Tokyo · Toronto · Zürich

Il presente volume è stato realizzato con il contributo di
The present volume has been made possible with assistance from

NEDERLANDSE ORGANISATIE VOOR WETENSCHAPPELIJK ONDERZOEK
STICHTUNG VOOR LITERATUUR-, MUZIEK- EN THEATERWETENSCHAP

MINISTERO PER I BENI E LE ATTIVITÀ CULTURALI – ROMA

EDIZIONE NAZIONALE ITALIANA DEGLI OPERA OMNIA
DI PIETRO ANTONIO LOCATELLI

PUBBLICATI IN COLLABORAZIONE CON
PUBLISHED IN ASSOCIATION WITH
STICHTING – FONDAZIONE
PIETRO ANTONIO LOCATELLI
AMSTERDAM – CREMONA

Performance material based on this edition is available from the publisher/
Der hier veröffentlichte Notentext is auch als Aufführungsmaterial beim Verlag erhältlich/
Le matériel d'éxecution réalisé à partir de cette édition est disponible auprès de l'éditeur
Eulenburg Orchestral Series: EOS 1887/1888/1889/1890

Ernst Eulenburg Ltd
48 Great Marlborough Street
London W1F 7BB

CONTENTS/INHALT

PREFACE

«*Most Illustrious and Excellent Sir. The honour I received during my stay in Venice of being graciously welcomed at your Excellency's house obliges me to express my gratitude with the present devout gesture of appreciation, by dedicating these concertos of mine to you, all the more so because you condescended to come and hear them, forgiving their faults, when I had them performed at those most celebrated functions by that excellent orchestra of unequalled number* [...]».

These were the words chosen by Pietro Antonio Locatelli (Bergamo, 1695 – Amsterdam, 1764), composer and violin virtuoso, when addressing the *«Venetian patrician»* Girolamo Michele Lin in his dedication of *L'Arte del Violino, XII Concerti, cioè Violino Solo, con XXIV Capricci ad Libitum*, Op. 3. Even though, to date, there is no documentary evidence that throws light on the actual place and real nature of the «most celebrated functions» (*famosissime fontioni*), Locatelli's statement suggests that these works were composed in the years 1723–1727, during the period when he was moving around in northern Italy: the first stage of a tour that was to take him to the main European musical centres and eventually conclude in Amsterdam in 1729. And it was there in Amsterdam, a few years later in 1733, that the collection was published by the printer Michel-Charles le Cène.

The first edition would have surely made a strong impression on its first purchasers, for with its 295 pages it was one of the celebrated publishing firm's most ambitious products. Moreover, its price of 25 gulden was the equivalent of a craftsman's average monthly wage. Evidently Le Cène, who was a shrewd businessman, immediately grasped the importance of a work whose extraordinarily innovative contents were destined to leave a significant mark on the history of music.

The twelve concertos are in three movements, ordered as fast-slow-fast. In accordance with the Vivaldian model, the outer movements consist of a succession of orchestral ritornelli (or tutti) that alternate with solo episodes in which the soloist is generally accompanied by the continuo only. The opening tutti is hardly ever repeated in its entirety during the intermediate expositions, but rather is constantly varied by juxtaposing the small 'motivic' groups that make up its musical substance. The final tutti, on the other hand, is often identical to the first, thereby conferring a sense of symmetry and completion on the movement. The distinctive element, however, of these outer movements is the inclusion of a capriccio for solo violin, to be played *ad libitum*. They are moments of bizarre, unstructured music of considerable length, placed before the final tutti and almost always followed by a cadenza left to improvisation. The singularity of Locatelli's capriccios lies in their length (sometimes exceeding that of the surrounding movement itself) and in the virtuosic momentum that pervades them. The middle movements contrast with the outer ones not only in pace, but also because they lack any clear organization of the musical material into distinct thematic blocks. There the writing acquires refinement and piquancy thanks to the harmonic tension imparted by frequent modulations and copious recourse to sevenths, suspensions, displaced resolutions and chromaticism.

In a historical perspective *L'Arte del Violino* owes its importance to the extraordinary emancipation of violin technique displayed. Among the more significant feats we should especially single out the use of hitherto unattempted positions. Considering that seventh position was already the limit contemplated in the contemporary theoretical literature, the frequent incursions into very high ranges that require seventeenth position are remarkable indeed. It is thought, moreover, that Locatelli's music was conceived for a violin equipped with a fingerboard that was longer than customary in his day — yet still not long enough to produce such high sounds, which were most likely obtained by pressing the strings outside the fingerboard.

Another significant feature of Locatelli's writing for the instrument is the way the fingers of the left hand are subjected to particularly wide extensions. Such extensions, which were impracticable for most violinists, were defined as 'hand splitting' by Francesco Galeazzi in his *Elementi teorico-pratici di musica con un saggio sopra l'arte di suonare il violino* (Rome, Pilucchi Chracas, 1791–1796). They are used both in the high register, with extensions of the fourth finger, and in the low, with contractions of the first finger; nor are the intermediate fingers exempt from similar exertions. By these means the very concept of 'position' is called into question.

The chordal technique is also of unparalleled complexity, if compared to the earlier and the contemporary violin literature. The playing of chords beyond seventh position requires absolute mastery of the bow and exceptional dexterity in the left hand, especially when the latter is burdened by further difficulties such as crossings, extensions, retractions of the fingers and changes of position. True virtuosity can be said to be achieved when the left hand and the right arm succeed in producing a smooth tone *en souplesse* in conjunction with rapid speeds of execution.

Finally, the violinist's expression of the musical argument must also be aided by a dextrous and varied art of the bow, subservient to the refinement of tone. Among the more common bowings we note the detaché bow (also combined with leaps and changes of string), staccato, spiccato and mixed bowing (consisting of detaché and slurred notes, at times played in combination with reversed bowing). To this summary list we should add the 'slurred staccato' bow, in which the staccato notes are to be played in the same bowstroke.

In consideration of the above, the *Arte del Violino* can be regarded as a genuine *Kunstbuch*. Moreover, its modernity was such that its ideal *continuum* – Niccolò Paganini's 24 Capricci, Op. 1 (c. 1820) – was produced almost a century later.

Capriccio 23 is given here both in its original version (as notated by Locatelli) and in a realization by Enzo Porta.

Cremona, Autumn 2003
Albert Dunning
Translation Hugh Ward-Perkins

VORWORT

«*Hochverehrtester und erlauchtester Herr. Die Ehre, die ich bei meinem Aufenthalt in Venedig hatte, freundlichst im Haus Ihrer Durchlaucht aufgenommen worden zu sein, drängt mich, meine Erkenntlichkeit darzutun durch das vorliegende, ergebene Zeichen meiner Dankbarkeit und Ihnen diese meine Concerti zu widmen; umso mehr, da Sie sich herabgelassen haben, dieselben zu hören und Anteil daran zu nehmen, als dieselben aus Anlass äußerst berühmter Festlichkeiten mit jenem tüchtigen und unerreichbar großen Orchester von mir zur Aufführung gebracht wurden.* [...]».

Mit diesen Worten wendet sich Pietro Antonio Locatelli (*1695 Bergamo – † 1764 Amsterdam) an den *«patricio veneto»* (*Patrizier aus Venedig*) Girolamo Michele Lin, dem die *Arte del Violino, XII Concerti, cioè Violino Solo, con XXIV Capricci ad Libitum* (*Kunst des Geigenspiels, 12 Konzerte, d.h. Violine solo, mit 24 Capricen ad libitum*), Opus 3 gewidmet sind. Auch wenn bis heute keine dokumentarischen Beweise vorliegen, die Klarheit schaffen, wo und in welchem Rahmen sich die *«famosissime fontioni»* (*äußerst berühmte Festlichkeiten*) abgespielt haben könnten, lassen die Worte des Komponisten und Geigenvirtuosen vermuten, dass das Werk in den Jahren 1723 bis 1727 entstand, als Locatelli sich nach Norditalien begab, erster Halt einer *Tour* durch die größten musikalischen Städte Europas bis nach Amsterdam, wo er 1729 ankam. Wenige Jahre später wurde die Sammlung dort vom Verleger Michel-Charles le Cène im Jahre 1733 in den Druck gegeben.

Die *Editio Princeps* muß großes Aufsehen erregt haben: mit seinen 295 Seiten erregte das Werk die Aufmerksamkeit des Publikums als eines der ehrgeizigsten Unternehmen des angesehenen Verlags – der Preis von 25 Florin entsprach übrigens dem durchschnittlichen Monatsgehalt eines Handwerkers. Offensichtlich hatte der erfahrene Le Cène sofort die Bedeutung des Werkes erkannt, deren wunderbar innovativer Inhalt dazu bestimmt war, eine wesentliche Spur in der Musikgeschichte zu hinterlassen.

Die 12 Konzerte bestehen aus drei Sätzen mit der Abfolge schnell-langsam-schnell. Die Außensätze bestehen nach Vivaldi-Manier aus abwechselnder Aufeinanderfolge von Orchester- (*Tutti*) und Soloabschnitten (*Solo*), in denen der Solist normalerweise vom Basso continuo begleitet wird. Das *Tutti* am Anfang wird in den Expositionen im Laufe des Satzes fast nie in seiner Gesamtheit wiederholt, taucht aber in veränderter Form in der Nebeneinanderstellung kleiner 'Motivgruppen' wieder auf, die die musikalische Substanz darstellen. Hingegen ist das letzte *Tutti* oft mit dem ersten identisch, um dem Satz Symmetrie und Schlüssigkeit zu verleihen. Das außergewöhnliche Moment der Außensätze jeden Konzertes besteht in der Einfügung eines Capriccios für Violine solo, das *ad libitum* ausgeführt wird: ein seltsames musikalisches Moment, das, unstrukturiert und nicht kurz, seinen Platz vor dem letzten *Tutti* findet und dem fast immer eine der Improvisation überlassene Kadenz folgt. Die Einzigartigkeit der Capricci von Locatelli liegt in ihrer Länge, die manchmal sogar über den Umfang des Satzes hinausgehen, indem sie angesiedelt sind, und in der virtuosen Wucht, die sie durchläuft. Die inneren Sätze unterscheiden sich von den äußeren nicht nur durch das Tempo, sondern auch durch das Fehlen einer klaren Anordnung des kompositorischen Materials in festgelegten, thematischen Blöcken. Der Stil wird so raffiniert und gewinnt an Würze dank der andauernden harmonischen Spannung, die sich aus häufigen Modulationen von Tonart zu Tonart und aus reichlichem Gebrauch von Septen, verspäteten Auflösungen, Trugschlüssen und Chromatik ergibt.

In geschichtlicher Hinsicht besteht die Bedeutung der *Arte del Violino* in der außergewöhnlichen Emanzipation der Violintechnik, deren Bote sie ist. Zu den wesentlichsten Eroberungen in diesem Sinne gehört zuallererst der Gebrauch der damals noch unerprobten Lagen. Die siebte Lage stellte die in den damaligen Lehrwerken propagierte Grenze dar, während häufige Ausflüge in sehr hohe Bereiche die siebzehnte Lage erforderlich machen. Man meint außerdem, dass die Stücke von Locatelli für eine Violine mit längerem Griffbrett als damals normal gedacht waren, das jedoch trotzdem immer noch nicht genügte, um so hohe Töne zu produzieren, die wahrscheinlich nur außerhalb des Griffbrettes gegriffen werden konnten.

Ein anderes wichtiges Element in den Kompositionen von Locatelli sind die großen Überstreckungen der linken Hand. Francesco Galeazzi definierte in seinen *Elementi teorico-pratici di musica con un saggio sopra l'arte di suonare il violino* (Roma, Pilucchi Chracas, 1791–1796) diese für die meisten Geiger unmöglichen Überstreckungen, nach oben hin mit Überstreckung des kleinen Fingers und nach unten durch die Zurückziehung des Zeigefingers, als «Handzerreißer»; die inneren Finger sind darüber hinaus auch an der Überstreckung beteiligt. Daraus ergibt sich, dass die Idee der Lage überholt ist.

Die Akkord-Technik wird immer komplizierter, nicht mehr vergleichbar mit der früheren und damals zeitgenössischen Geigenliteratur. Die Ausführung von Akkorden, die über die siebte Lage hinausgehen, erfordert eine absolute Bogenkontrolle und eine außergewöhnliche Gewandtheit der linken Hand, die zumal noch andere Schwierigkeiten zu bewältigen hat, wie komplizierte Fingerstellungen, Überstreckungen, Zurückziehen der Finger und Lagenwechsel. Die Virtuosität ist dann zu erkennen, wenn die linke Hand und der rechte Arm es auch in schnellem Tempo schaffen, *en souplesse* einen optimalen Ton zu erzeugen.

Letztendlich nimmt eine wissende und vielfältige Bogenkunst, der Klangsuche zu Diensten, Anteil an einer ausdrucksvollen Tonsprache. Unter den häufigsten Bogenstrichen sind der Strich ohne Bindung, auch kombiniert mit Saitensprüngen und Saitenwechseln, das Stakkato, der Wurfbogen, kombinierte Stricharten mit ungebundenen und gebundenen Noten, die bisweilen im Gegenbogen auszuführen sind, zu erwähnen. Bleibt noch die Strichart des gebundenen Stakkatos hinzuzufügen, bei der die gestoßenen Noten auf demselben Bogenstrich ausgeführt werden.

In Anbetracht der angestellten Ausführungen ist *Die Kunst des Geigenspiels* als *Kunstbuch*[1] anzusehen.

Die vielfältig modernen Züge des Werkes op. 3 waren dafür verantwortlich, dass schon ein Jahrhundert später die ideale Fortsetzung verfasst wurde: es handelt sich um die 24 Capricci, op. 1 (um 1820) von Niccolò Paganini.

Das Capriccio 23 wird sowohl in der Originalversion, wie von Locatelli aufgeschrieben, als auch in der Ausführung von Enzo Porta vorgelegt.

Crémone, Herbst 2003
Albert Dunning
Übersetzung Ursula Schaa

[1] Auf Deutsch im italienischen Originaltext.

INTRODUZIONE

«Ill.mo et Ecc.mo Signore. L'honore che hò ricevuto nel mio soggiorno in Venezia d'essere stato benignamente accolto in Casa di vostra Eccellenza, mi obbliga a testificarle la mia riconoscenza con il presente divoto officio di gratitudine, nel dedicarle questi miei Concerti, tanto più che s'è Lei degnata di venire ad udirli, e compatirli, quando in coteste famosissime fontioni con quella valorosa e senza pari numerosissima Orchestra sono stati da me posti in essecutione. [...]».

Con queste espressioni, Pietro Antonio Locatelli (Bergamo, 1695 – Amsterdam, 1764) si rivolge al *«patricio veneto»* Girolamo Michele Lin, dedicatario dell'*Arte del Violino, XII Concerti, cioè Violino Solo, con XXIV Capricci ad Libitum*, Op. III. Sebbene, a tutt'oggi, non vi siano prove documentarie che facciano luce sull'ambientazione e la natura delle *«famosissime fontioni»*, le parole del compositore e virtuoso del violino inducono a datare la stesura dell'Opera agli anni 1723–1727, allorché Locatelli si mosse nel settentrione d'Italia, prima meta di un *tour* che lo portò nei maggiori centri musicali europei e che si concluse ad Amsterdam, nel 1729. Lì, pochi anni dopo, la raccolta venne data alle stampe, per i tipi di Michel-Charles le Cène; era il 1733.

L'*editio princeps* dovette destare grande scalpore: con le sue 295 pagine si imponeva all'attenzione del pubblico come una delle più ambiziose imprese editoriali della prestigiosa casa editrice – il prezzo di 25 fiorini, peraltro, corrispondeva al salario medio mensile di un artigiano. È evidente che lo scaltrito Le Cène ebbe subito chiara l'importanza dell'Opera, i cui contenuti straordinariamente innovativi erano destinati a lasciare un segno significativo nella storia della musica.

I 12 Concerti sono strutturati in tre tempi disposti in successione veloce-lento-veloce. I movimenti estremi si articolano, sul calco vivaldiano, secondo un alterno susseguirsi di episodi orchestrali (o Tutti) ed episodi solistici (Solo), nei quali il solista suona, solitamente, accompagnato dal basso continuo. Il Tutti d'apertura non viene quasi mai ripetuto integralmente nelle esposizioni intermedie, riproponendosi, piuttosto, variato nella giustapposizione dei piccoli gruppi 'motivici' che ne informano la sostanza musicale. Di contro, il Tutti conclusivo è spesso identico al primo, in modo da conferire simmetria e compiutezza al movimento. L'elemento peculiare dei tempi estremi di ciascun Concerto è rappresentato da un Capriccio per violino solo da eseguirsi *ad libitum*: momento musicale bizzarro, destrutturato, di non breve durata, si colloca prima del Tutti finale ed è quasi sempre seguito da una Cadenza lasciata all'improvvisazione. La singolarità dei Capricci locatelliani sta nella lunghezza, talora maggiore del movimento che li incorpora, e nello spiccato empito virtuosistico che li pervade. I movimenti centrali contrastano con quelli esterni sia per l'agogica sia per l'assenza di una chiara organizzazione del materiale musicale in blocchi tematici definiti. La scrittura diviene così ricercata, acquistando sapidità grazie all'esasperazione della tensione armonica perseguita attraverso frequenti modulazioni intratonali e un copioso impiego di settime, ritardi, risoluzioni evitate, cromatismi.

In prospettiva storica, l'importanza dell'*Arte del Violino* è da vedersi nella straordinaria emancipazione della tecnica violinistica di cui è latrice. Tra le conquiste più significative in tal senso si pone, *in primis*, l'utilizzo di posizioni al tempo intentate. Considerando che la settima posizione costituiva il limite contemplato nella trattatistica coeva, le frequenti incursioni in tessiture sopracute impongono il raggiungimento della diciassettesima posizione. Si pensa, peraltro, che la scrittura locatelliana abbia fatto riferimento a un violino dotato di una tastiera allungata rispetto ai canoni dell'epoca e tuttavia ancora insufficiente per produrre suoni tanto acuti, ottenuti, verosimilmente, tastando le corde al di fuori della stessa.

Un altro elemento di rilievo della scrittura locatelliana è costituito dalle grandi estensioni alle quali sono sottoposte le dita della mano. Francesco Galeazzi, nei suoi *Elementi teorico-pratici di musica con un saggio sopra l'arte di suonare il violino* (Roma, Pilucchi Chracas, 1791–1796), definì *«squarci di mano»* quelle estensioni impraticabili per la maggioranza dei violinisti, attuate sia all'acuto, con l'estensione del mignolo, sia al grave, con la ritrazione dell'indice; le dita intermedie non si sottraggono, inoltre, a simili sollecitazioni. Ne consegue, talora, il superamento del concetto di posizione.

La tecnica accordale assume una complessità senza paragoni se raffrontata alla letteratura violinistica anteriore e coeva. L'esecuzione di accordi posti oltre la settima posizione esige un'assoluta padronanza dell'arco e un'eccezionale destrezza della mano sinistra, allorché quest'ultima sia gravata da ulteriori difficoltà quali incroci, estensioni, ritrazioni delle dita e cambi di posizione. Il virtuosismo emerge quando la mano sinistra e il braccio destro riescono a rendere *en souplesse* un suono levigato in concomitanza di una velocità d'esecuzione sostenuta.

Infine, una sapiente e varia arte dell'arco, asservita alla ricercatezza del suono, concorre all'espressività del discorso musicale. Tra le arcate più comuni si registrano il colpo d'arco sciolto, applicato pure in combinazione con salti e cambi di corda, lo staccato, lo spiccato, l'arcata mista, comprendente note sciolte e legate da eseguirsi a volte in contrarco. Alla rapida rassegna si aggiunge il legato-staccato, la cui esecuzione comporta che le note staccate si suonino con il medesimo colpo d'arco.

In considerazione di quanto esposto, l'*Arte del Violino* assurge al rango di un *Kunstbuch*.

La modernità dell'Op. III fu tale che solo a distanza di un secolo ne venne composto l'ideale *continuum*: si tratta dei 24 Capricci, Op. I (ca. 1820), di Niccolò Paganini.

Il Capriccio 23 viene proposto sia nella versione originale, ossia così come notato da Locatelli, sia nella realizzazione di Enzo Porta.

Cremona, autunno 2003
Albert Dunning

INTRODUCTION

«Illustrissime et excellentissime seigneur. L'honneur que j'ai reçu lors de mon séjour à Venise ayant été accueilli avec bienveillance dans la Maison de Votre Excellence, m'oblige à vous témoigner ma reconnaissance avec la ci-présente expression dévouée de gratitude, en vous dédiant ces Concerts, d'autant plus que Vous avez daigné venir les écouter, et les agréer, au moment où, dans ces célèbre fonctions et avec le concours de cet Orchestre de grande valeur, exceptionnellement nombreux, ils ont été proposés par moi-même à l'execution. [...]».

C'est avec ces expressions que Pietro Antonio Locatelli (Bergame, 1695 –Amsterdam, 1764) s'adresse au *«patricio veneto»* («patricien vénitien») Girolamo Michele Lin, dédicataire de l'*Arte del Violino, XII Concerti, cioè Violino Solo, con XXIV Capricci ad Libitum* (L'Art du Violon, Douze Concerts à Violon Solo, avec 24 Caprices au choix), Opus III. Bien que nous ne disposions toujours pas de témoignages documentaires qui nous permettent d'avoir des lumières sur les circonstance et sur la nature des «fonctions» (*«famosissime fontioni»*) évoquées, les paroles du compositeur et virtuose du violon nous amènent à dater la rédaction de cet Opus autour des années 1723–1727, au moment où Locatelli de déplaça dans le Nord de l'Italie: une première étape d'une longue pérégrination qui le conduisit vers les principaux centres musicaux européens, et qui arriva à sa conclusion à Amsterdam, en 1729. C'est dans cette capitale, quelques années plus tard, que cette oeuvre fut imprimée, par les soins de Michel-Charles le Cène; c'était l'annnée 1733.

L'édition princeps dut faire grand bruit: avec ses 295 pages, elle s'imposait à l'attention du public comme un des exploits les plus audacieux de cette prestigieuse maison d'édition; le prix de 25 florins correspondait d'aillleurs au salaire mensuel moyen d'un artisan. Il est évident que Le Cène, toujours adroit, se rendit compte immédiatement de l'importance de cette Oeuvre dont le contenu, par ses extraordinaires caractéristiques d'innovation, était destiné à laisser une trace significative dans l'histoire de la musique.

Les Douze Concerts sont structurés en trois mouvements, disposés dans l'ordre rapide-lent-rapide. Les mouvements aux extrêmes s'articulent – suivant le modèle de Vivaldi – en une succession alternée d'épisodes de l'orchestre tout entier (*Tutti*) et d'épisodes du soliste (*Solo*), dans lesquels ce dernier joue accompagné, d'ordinaire, seulement par la basse continue. Le premier *Tutti* au début des concerts n'est presque jamais répété intégralement dans les reprises intermédiaires, tout au long du mouvement, mais il réapparaît plutôt en forme variée par la juxtaposition des petits groupes des 'motifs' musicaux qui en composent le matériau musical. Par contre, le *Tutti* conclusif est souvent identique au premier, de manière à donner de la symétrie et un sens d'achèvement au mouvement. L'élément caractéristique des mouvements rapides de chaque Concert est représenté par un *Capriccio* (Caprice) pour le violon seul à jouer *ad libitum*: il s'agit d'un moment musical bizarre, déstructuré, de durée plutôt longue, qui se place juste avant le *Tutti* final et qui est presque toujours suivi par une *Cadenza* laissée à l'improvisation. La singularité des *Capricci* de Locatelli est d'ailleurs aussi dans leur ampleur, parfois plus importante même du mouvement entier à l'intérieur duquel ils se placent, mais aussi dans le puissant élan de virtuosisme qui les caractérise. Les mouvement lents, centrals, contrastent avec les rapides, à la fois par leur agogique comme par l'absence d'une organisation claire du matériau musical en blocs tématiques bien définis. L'écriture devient donc recherchée, en gagnant encore en originalité grâce à l'exaspération des tensions harmoniques créées par de nombreuses modulations intratonales et en faisant recours largement aux septièmes, aux retards, aux résolutions évitées, aux chromatismes.

Du point de vue historique, l'importance de l'*Arte del Violino* doit être recherchée dans la formidable émancipation de la technique du violon que cette oeuvre témoigne. Dans ce cadre, parmi les conquêtes plus considérables, il faut évoquer tout d'abord le recours à des positions encore inexploitées à cette époque. Il faut rappeler que la septième position était déjà la limite prévue par les traités de ces mêmes années, et les nombreuses incursions de Locatelli vers les tessitures suraigües imposent d'atteindre au moins la dix-septième position. On pense d'ailleurs que cette écriture doive se rapporter à un violon muni d'une touche rallongée par rapport à l'usage du temps et, pourtant, encore insuffisante pour produire des sons aussi aigus, obtenus, vraisemblablement, en touchant les cordes au-delà de la touche.

Un autre élément fort important dans l'écriture de Locatelli concerne les grandes extensions que doivent endurer les doigts de la main. Dans ses *Elementi teorico-pratici di musica con un saggio sopra l'arte di suonare il violino* [*Éléments théoriques et pratiques de musique, avec un essai sur l'art de jouer le violon*] (Roma, Pilucchi Chracas, 1791–1796), Francesco Galeazzi definit come *«squarci di mano»* [«déchirures de la main»] ces extensions impossibles à réaliser pour la plupart des violonistes, à la fois vers l'aigu, avec l'extension du petit doigt, comme vers le grave, en rétractant l'index; les autres doigts ne peuvent d'ailleurs se soustraire à des contraintes semblables. Il en résulte, à l'occasion, le dépassement du concept commun de position.

La technique du jeu par accords atteint un niveau de complexité sans pareil si on la compare au répertoire pour le violon de la même époque ou précédent. La réalisation d'accords au-delà de la septième position exige le contrôle absolu de l'archet et une agilité exceptionnelle de la main gauche, en particulier lorsqu'elle est soumise à bien d'autres difficultés telles que le croisement, l'extension ou la rétraction des doigts et les changements de position. La virtuosité se réalise lorsque la main gauche et le bras droit réussissent à rendre en souplesse un son bien poli, tout en soutenant une vitesse d'execution de grande vivacité.

Enfin, l'art de l'archet, aussi savant que varié et asservi à la recherche et au raffinement du son, concourt à l'expressivité du discours musical. Parmi les coups d'archet plus courants, il faut noter le coup d'archet délié, appliqué, même combiné aux sauts et aux changements de corde, le *staccato*, détaché (*spiccato*), le coup d'archet mixte, comprenant des notes déliées et liées à réaliser parfois en 'poussé'. À ce bref échantillon il faut ajouter le *legato-staccato*, dont l'exécution exige que les notes détachées (en *staccato*) soient jouées sur le même coup d'archet.

En considérant tout ce qui a été évoqué, l'*Arte del Violino* s'élève sans aucun doute au rang d'un véritable *Kunstbuch*.

La modernité de l'Opus III fut telle que seulement un siècle plus tard parut sa continuation idéale: les 24 *Capricci*, Op. I (ca. 1820), composés par Niccolò Paganini.

Le Capriccio 23 est proposé à la fois dans sa version originale, c'est à dire tel qu'il a été noté par Locatelli, et dans la réalisation de Enzo Porta.

Crémone, automne 2003
Albert Dunning
Traduction de Daniel Torelli

L'ARTE DEL VIOLINO

Pietro Antonio Locatelli
(1695–1764)

CONCERTO V

Op. 3/5–8

Edited by Albert Dunning

17

20

23

solo
solo
tasto solo

[tutti]
tutti
solo
solo

55
tr
6 5 9 4 8 3 6 5 9 4 8 6 3 7 6 7 6

58
tr

62
tutti
tr
[f]
f
tutti

66
tr
69
tr
72
p
f
CAPRICCIO (9)

[violino solo]
p
f

tr
6
Cadenza

142
tutti
tr
f
5
6
7
144
p
6
[p]
[f]
4
3
Adagio
solo
pp

9
Allegro
tr
organo f
8
6
5
4
3
#
7

16
b7
7
24
7
32
solo
tutti
p
f
6
5

42
solo
[tutti]
[solo]
f
f
f
[f]
51
[tutti]
[solo]
[tutti]
[solo]
[f]
f
f
[f]
[f]
solo
6
6
58
tr
p
p
p
6
[p]
4 [♯]3

tutti
65
tr
[tr]
tr
f
f
f
tutti
[f]
74
82

90
solo
p
p
7
#
7
#
100
tutti
solo
f
p
f
p
f
solo
tutti
f
6
5
#
#
#4
2
7
#
7
#
6
5
#
7
#
108
tr
tr
tr
solo
7
#
6
7
#

114
tr
tr
tr
tr
p
p
120
tutti
solo
tr
tr
f
f
tutti
solo
127
tr
tr
f
f
f
tutti

132
137
solo
145
tutti
tr
tutti
[tr]
p
f

CAPRICCIO (10)
[violino solo]
tr

220
223
226
tr
232
235
239
243
246
249
CADENZA
251
tutti
f
[f]
6
5
6
4
3

Concerto VI

Largo
Violino solo
Violino I
Violino II
Viola
Violoncello solo
Basso
Andante
soli
tutti
solo
[f]
tr
p
11

15
soli
tr
p
solo
soli
20
tutti
solo
f
tutti
p
24

28
tr
tr
tr
tr
tr
32
tr
tr
tr
tr
tr
36
tr

39
tr
p
pp
[p]
6 4
5 3
b6 4
43
f
tutti
[f]
9 7
8 6
47
soli
solo
#6

tutti
solo
tutti
tutti
tutti
solo
tasto solo
tutti
solo
tasto solo
tutti
solo
tutti
solo

61
tr
tr
tutti
tr
tr
tr
tr
solo
f
tutti
solo
tutti
tutti
♭6
♭6
♯4
2
6
♭7
♭6
5
♯
9
7
8
♯6
6
5
7
9
8
65
8
6
7
5
6
4
5
♯3
70
p
solo
solo
solo
♯4
2
6
7
♭
♭7

74
a due violini
f
p
tutti
tasto solo
78
tutti
[tutti]
tasto solo
82
pp
tr
Adagio

Capriccio (11)

190
198
206
214
222
230
238
246
254
262
269
273
tr

277
tutti
tr
f
282
p
Adagio
solo
solo
pp
1.
2.

10
1.
2.
VIVACE
solo
tutti
tr
solo
p
f
11
tutti
tr
soli
solo
soli

20
tutti
soli
tutti
soli
f
tutti
solo
tutti
solo
f
tutti
soli
tutti
soli
27
tutti
solo
tutti
tutti
p
p
35
p
tutti
tr
tr
f
tr
[f]

solo
solo
p
tr

72
tr
tr

80

87
tr
tr
tr
tr

94
tr
tutti
solo
[tutti] tr
tr
f
p
f
p
f
f
f
tutti
4 [♯]3
6
6
103
soli
tutti
soli
solo
tutti
solo
soli
tutti
soli
5
5
110
tutti
solo
[f]
tutti
solo
f
tutti
solo
tutti
solo
6
♭6
6
6

117
tutti
tr
solo
tr
tutti
tr
p
p
p
tutti
6 ♭ ♭7
solo
4
2
tutti
♯
[p]
♯
6 ♭ ♭7
p ♯
♯
125
6
5
♭
6
5
♭
6
♭5
6
5
♭
6
5
♭
6
♭5
130
6
♭5
6
5
6
♭5
6
5

135
140
145
p
f
[f]
6
5

155
tutti
tr
f
p
6 7
5 5
CAPRICCIO (12)
[violino solo]
165
169
173
177
182
187
192
197

202
206
210
213
217
221
225
229
233
237
241
245

249
p
pp
p
f
253
257
261
Cadenza
tutti
solo
organo f
267
tutti
tr

Concerto VII

21
tr
solo
8
6
p

solo
pp
pp

37
tutti
f
f
tutti
41
45
solo
tr
p
p

48
solo
52
56

60
tutti
tr
solo
tr
p
f
p
f
p
f
tutti
solo
63
tr
tutti
tr
solo
tr
p
f
p
f
p
f
tutti
solo
67
tr
p
p

70
73
76
tr
tutti
p
p
f
f
[f]
tutti

79
82
85
tr
p
f
[f]

Capriccio (13)
[violino solo]

CADENZA

163
tutti
f
f
[f]
f
f
4 3 6 ♭5 4
4 3 6 ♭5 4 3
166
6
5
4 3 6 ♭5 4
4 3 6 ♭5 4 3
LARGO
solo
tutti
p
♭7
5
[♭]6 5
4 3
9 8
4 3
[p]

5
tutti
solo
tutti
solo
9
tutti
solo
tutti
13

17
pp
f
p
solo
tr
23
30
tutti
[f]
p
[p]

35
solo
tr
tr
solo
♭6
4
6
5
9
♭
8
6
♭4
6
[♭]5
9
6
4
3
9
8

42
tr
♯
♯4
2
6
6
5
♭6
[♭]7
6
7
6
7
♯
7
5

49
tr
tutti
p
[f]
p
[f]
p
solo
tutti
solo
[f]
p
tutti
[f]
6
4
5
4
[♯]3
♭7
5
[♭]6
4
5
3
♯
6
5
[p]
9
4
8
3
[f]
♭7
5
[♭]6
4
5
3
♯
6
5
p
9
4
8
3

54
tutti
solo
tutti
58
62
tr
tr

Allegro
ottave sole
ottave sole
8
15

24
32
40

47
soli
solo
solo
solo
soli
tr
55
tutti
tutti
p
p
7 6
6
6
6 5
4 3
62
6
6
6

69
tr
tutti
p
6
5
tasto solo
78
solo
tutti
4 3
ottave sole
86
5 6
7 6
7 6
7 6
7 6
7 6
6

94
solo
solo
f
f
f
[f]
p
p
102
tutti
tutti
f
f
111
solo
solo

119
tutti
tr
solo
3
tutti
solo
7
4
3
127
tutti
solo
tr
p
tutti
6
135
solo
f
tasto solo

143
tr
tr
tr
[tr]
tr
4

150
tr
tutti
tutti
tutti
tutti
tutti
ottave sole
ottave sole

158

166
174
CAPRICCIO (14)
182
[violino solo]
186
190
194

tr

244
248
251
255
Cadenza
259
tutti
f
f
f
f ottave sole
ottave sole
organo f
267
tr

Concerto VIII

13
tr
solo
f
17
p
solo
21
tutti
[p] tasto solo
p tasto solo

24
tr
f
[f]6
27
p
solo
31
tr

34
tr
37
tr
40
tr
tr

43
tutti
f
f
[f]
[f]
[f]
46
49

52
p
f
6
6 5 ♯ 6 [p]
[f]
♯6
6 5 ♯ 6 p
55
solo
[♯]3
59

tutti
tasto solo
[p]
tasto solo
[f]
[f]

CAPRICCIO (15)
[violino solo]

Cadenza

137
tutti
f
p
tasto solo
[p]
140
tr
[f]
[f]6
f6
143
[#]3

Largo
7
p
f
solo
sempre p
13

19
tr
25
tutti
p
f
solo
[tutti]
sempre p
31

37
tr
43
tr
tutti
[tutti]
49

Allegro
p
f
tr
soli
solo

22
tutti
tutti
tutti
tutti
28
solo
34
tutti

40
8 7 6 5
6 5 4 [♯]3
p
46
solo
f
[f]♯
52
solo

58
tr
p
contrabbasso solo senza cembalo
64
tr
70

75
tr
81
tutti
f
f
tutti
tutti
87
tr
tr

93
tr
6
9 8
6
99
solo
105
solo
f

111
p
p
p
6
6
4
5
♯3
♯
117
123
solo

129
tutti
tutti
solo
tutti
tutti
135
141

147
solo
tutti
152
157

Capriccio (16)
[violino solo]
163
165
167
169
172
175
177
179
181
183
185
187

189
191
195
199
202
205
208
211
213
216
218
tr

CADENZA
tutti
organo